MUG *crumbles*

Ready in 3 minutes in the microwave!

Christelle Huet–Gomez
Photography by David Japy

hardie grant books

Contents

making mug crumbles..4

APPLE MUG CRUMBLES

cinnamon & apple mug crumble 6

apple & caramel mug crumble 8

pecan & apple mug crumble............................. 10

apple, dried fruit & nut mug crumble............... 12

Carambar® & apple mug crumble................... 14

FRUIT MUG CRUMBLES

rhubarb, apple & almond mug crumble............ 16

blackberry & apple mug crumble 18

apricot, apple & pistachio mug crumble.......... 20

banana, apple & coconut mug crumble........... 22

raspberry, apple & matcha tea mug
crumble 24

CHOCOLATE MUG CRUMBLES

vanilla, apple & chocolate mug crumble 26

choc-nut & apple mug crumble......................... 28

raspberry, apple & white chocolate
mug crumble 30

pear & chocolate mug crumble 32

cherry, apple & chocolate mug crumble 34

strawberry, apple & double-choc mug
crumble 36

pear with gingerbread & white chocolate
mug crumble 38

ganache mug crumble....................................... 40

CREAMY MUG CRUMBLES

pear & chestnut purée mug crumble 42

fig, apple, yoghurt & hazelnut mug crumble 44

blueberry & lemon curd mug crumble 46

red berries, apple, lemon & cream cheese mug
crumble 48

banana, apple & peanut mug crumble 50

BISCUITY MUG CRUMBLES

pineapple, apple & caramelised biscuit mug
crumble 52

red berries, apple & shortbread mug crumble ...54

damson plum & apple with Breton butter biscuits
mug crumble 56

mirabelle plum, apple & shortbread mug
crumble 58

raspberry, apple & pink-wafer biscuit mug
crumble 60

peach & strawberry biscotti mug crumble 62

SAVOURY MUG CRUMBLES

salmon with courgette & hazelnut mug
crumble 64

cherry tomatoes with three cheeses mug
crumble 66

courgette & feta with polenta mug crumble 68

olive, tomato & Parmesan mug crumble............70

notes on the recipes 72

acknowledgements 72

making mug crumbles

The mug crumble is a soft crumble ready in 5 minutes. The only equipment you need are a mug, a spoon and a microwave.

No weighing needed

The quantities in the recipes are given in spoonfuls. If you need to adapt these, check the table of equivalents at the end of the book.

Perfect crumbles

To get crunchy crumbles, you need to mix the dough with the tips of your fingers (not with a spoon) to obtain a fine consistency, with the ingredients well combined. Crumble it over the fruit then cook in the microwave for the time stated in the recipe.

Cooking: 3 minutes in the microwave

When cooking the fruit, cover the mug with cling film (plastic wrap) pierced with a few holes to avoid any spattering.

Microwaves vary from one another, so it may be necessary to reduce or increase the cooking time by a few seconds according to the results of your first try.

These are generous recipes. For smaller portions, divide the amount of fruit in half without changing the quantity of crumble. The cooking times remain the same.

Important: never put metal mugs or old cups in the microwave.

Eat them straight away

You can eat your mug crumble straight from the cup with a teaspoon when it begins to cool. That's the best moment! It will not keep once cooled.

....

cinnamon & apple mug crumble

FRUIT
2 apples, peeled, cored and diced
1 tablespoon caster (superfine) sugar
1 teaspoon ground cinnamon
a knob of butter

CRUMBLE
1 slice of butter 5 mm (¼ in) thick
  (15 g/½ oz)
1 tablespoon soft brown sugar
1 teaspoon ground cinnamon
3 tablespoons plain (all-purpose) flour
a pinch of salt

In a mug: mix the apple with the sugar, cinnamon and butter. Cover the mug with cling film (plastic wrap) pierced several times.

Cook in the microwave for 2 minutes at 800 watts or 1 minute 30 seconds at 1000 watts. Pour off any excess liquid.

In a bowl, mix the butter, soft brown sugar, cinnamon, flour and salt with your fingertips to form a dough.

Crumble it into the mug and cook in the microwave for 1 minute 30 seconds at 800 watts or 1 minute 10 seconds at 1000 watts.

Leave to cool a little before eating.

apple & caramel

mug crumble

FRUIT
2 apples, peeled,
   cored and diced
1 tablespoon caster
   (superfine) sugar
1 teaspoon natural
   vanilla extract
a knob of butter

CRUMBLE
1 slice of butter 5 mm
   (¼ in) thick (15 g/½ oz)
1 tablespoon soft brown sugar
2 tablespoons liquid
   caramel or 1 tablespoom
   of dulche de leche
3 heaped tablespoons
   plain (all-purpose) flour
a pinch of salt

In a mug: mix the apple with the sugar, vanilla and butter. Cover the mug with cling film (plastic wrap) pierced several times.

Cook in the microwave for 1 minute at 800 watts or 50 seconds at 1000 watts. Pour off any excess liquid and stir again.

In a bowl, mix the butter, soft brown sugar, 1 tablespoon of the caramel, the flour and salt with your fingertips to form a dough.

Crumble it into the mug and cook in the microwave for 2 minutes at 800 watts or 1 minute 30 seconds at 1000 watts. Pour the remaining caramel over the crumble before eating .

FOR 1 MUG – 5 MINUTES (PREP + COOK)

pecan & apple
mug crumble

FRUIT
2 apples, peeled,
  cored and diced
1 tablespoon caster
  (superfine) sugar
a knob of butter
1 tablespoon maple syrup

CRUMBLE
1 tablespoon chopped
  pecan nuts
1 slice of butter 5 mm
  (¼ in) thick (15 g/½ oz)
1 tablespoon soft brown sugar
3 heaped tablespoons
  plain (all-purpose) flour
a pinch of salt
1 tablespoon maple syrup

In a mug: mix the apple with the sugar and butter.
Cover the mug with cling film (plastic wrap) pierced
several times.

Cook in the microwave for 1 minute at 800 watts or
50 seconds at 1000 watts. Pour off any excess liquid.
Add the maple syrup and stir again.

In a bowl, mix the butter, soft brown sugar, pecan nuts,
flour and salt with your fingertips to form a dough.

Crumble it into the mug and cook in the microwave for
2 minutes at 800 watts or 1 minute 30 seconds at 1000
watts. Pour the maple syrup over the crumble before eating.

*Tip: For an even tastier mug crumble, dry toast the pecans in
a frying pan for about 5 minutes.*

FOR 1 MUG – 5 MINUTES (PREP + COOK)

10 - *apple mug crumbles*

apple, dried fruit & nut mug crumble

FRUIT

2 apples, peeled, cored and diced
1 tablespoon caster (superfine) sugar
a knob of butter
1 tablespoon raisins
1 tablespoon dried cranberries
1 tablespoon toasted flaked almonds

CRUMBLE

1 slice of butter 5 mm
 (¼ in) thick (15 g/½ oz)
1 tablespoon soft brown sugar
2 tablespoons oat flakes
1 heaped tablespoon plain
 (all-purpose) flour
a pinch of salt
1 tablespoon toasted flaked almonds

In a mug: mix the apple with the sugar and butter. Cover the mug with cling film (plastic wrap) pierced several times.

Cook in the microwave for 1 minute at 800 watts or 50 seconds at 1000 watts. Pour off any excess liquid. Add the dried fruit and nuts and stir again.

In a bowl, mix the butter, soft brown sugar, oat flakes, flour and salt with your fingertips to form a dough.

Crumble it into the mug and cook in the microwave for 1 minute 30 seconds at 800 watts or 1 minute 10 seconds at 1000 watts. Sprinkle the flaked almonds over the crumble before eating.

Carambar® & apple

mug crumble

FRUIT
2 apples, peeled,
   cored and diced
3 Carambars®, cut into pieces
1 tablespoon single
   (light) cream

CRUMBLE
1 slice of butter 5 mm
   (¼ in) thick (15 g/½ oz)
1 teaspoon soft brown sugar
2 heaped tablespoons
   plain (all-purpose) flour
a pinch of salt
1 Carambar®, cut into pieces

In a mug: mix the apple with the pieces of Carambar®.
Cover the mug with cling film (plastic wrap) pierced several
times.

Cook in the microwave for 1 minute at 800 watts
or 50 seconds at 1000 watts. Pour off any excess liquid. Add
the cream and stir again.

In a bowl, mix the butter, soft brown sugar, flour and salt
with your fingertips to form a dough.

Crumble this dough into the mug. Sprinkle the pieces of
Carambar® on top and cook in the microwave for 1 minute
30 seconds at 800 watts or 1 minute 10 seconds at 1000
watts. Let it cool a little before eating.

FOR 1 MUG – 5 MINUTES (PREP + COOK)

14 - *apple mug crumbles*

rhubarb, apple & almond mug crumble

FRUIT

1 apple, peeled, cored and diced
generous ½ cup (70 g/2½ oz)
   rhubarb, peeled and diced
1 tablespoon vanilla sugar
a knob of butter

CRUMBLE

1 slice of butter 5 mm
   (¼ in) thick (15 g/½ oz)
1 heaped tablespoon soft brown sugar
2 heaped tablespoons
   plain (all-purpose) flour
1 tablespoon flaked almonds
a pinch of salt

In a mug: mix the apple with the rhubarb, sugar and butter. Cover the mug with cling film (plastic wrap) pierced several times.

Cook in the microwave for 1 minute at 800 watts or 50 seconds at 1000 watts. Pour off any excess liquid. Stir, cover with cling film pierced several times and cook again for 1 minute at 800 watts or 50 seconds at 1000 watts.

In a bowl, mix the butter, soft brown sugar, flour, flaked almonds and salt with your fingertips to form a dough.

Crumble it into the mug and cook in the microwave for 1 minute 30 seconds at 800 watts or 1 minute 10 seconds at 1000 watts.

Leave to cool a little before eating.

TIP: For an even tastier mug crumble, dry toast the almonds in a frying pan for about 5 minutes.

....

blackberry & apple mug crumble

FRUIT
1 apple, peeled, cored and diced
1 heaped tablespoon caster
  (superfine) sugar
a knob of butter
generous ½ cup (80 g/3 oz) blackberries

CRUMBLE
1 slice of butter 5 mm
  (¼ in) thick (15 g/½ oz)
1 teaspoon soft brown sugar
2 tablespoons runny honey
2 heaped tablespoons plain
  (all-purpose) flour
a pinch of salt

In a mug: mix the apple with the sugar and butter. Cover the mug with cling film (plastic wrap) pierced several times.

Cook in the microwave for 1 minute at 800 watts or 50 seconds at 1000 watts. Pour off any excess liquid. Add the blackberries and stir again.

In a bowl, mix the butter, sugar, 1 tablespoon of the honey, the flour and salt with your fingertips to form a dough.

Crumble it into the mug and cook in the microwave for 1 minute at 800 watts or 1 minute 10 seconds at 1000 watts. Pour the remaining honey over the crumble and let it cool a little before eating.

....

apricot, apple & pistachio mug crumble

FRUIT

1 apple, peeled, cored and diced

3 apricots, pitted and diced

1 tablespoon caster (superfine) sugar

a knob of butter

CRUMBLE

1 slice of butter 5 mm
  (¼ in) thick (15 g/½ oz)

1 tablespoon soft brown sugar

1 heaped tablespoon plain
  (all-purpose) flour

1 heaped tablespoon ground pistachios

a pinch of salt

In a mug: mix the apple and apricot with the sugar and butter. Cover the mug with cling film (plastic wrap) pierced several times.

Cook in the microwave for 1 minute at 800 watts or 50 seconds at 1000 watts. Pour off any excess liquid and stir again.

In a bowl, mix the butter, soft brown sugar, flour, ground pistachios and salt with your fingertips to form a dough.

Crumble it into the mug and cook in the microwave for 2 minutes at 800 watts or 1 minute 30 seconds at 1000 watts.

Let it cool a little before eating.

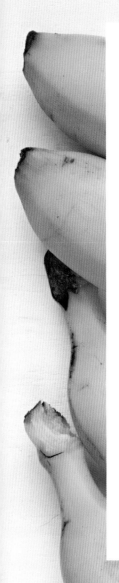

banana, apple & coconut

mug crumble

FRUIT

1 apple, peeled,
  cored and diced
½ banana, sliced into rounds
1 tablespoon caster
  (superfine) sugar
a knob of butter
1 teaspoon rum

CRUMBLE

1 slice of butter 5 mm
  (¼ in) thick (15 g/½ oz)
1 heaped tablespoon
  soft brown sugar
1 tablespoon desiccated
  (grated dried) coconut
1 heaped tablespoon
  plain (all-purpose) flour
a pinch of salt

In a mug: mix the apple with the banana, sugar and butter. Cover the mug with cling film (plastic wrap) pierced several times.

Cook in the microwave for 1 minute at 800 watts or 50 seconds at 1000 watts. Pour off any excess liquid. Add the rum and stir again.

In a bowl, mix the butter, soft brown sugar, coconut, flour and salt with your fingertips to form a dough.

Crumble it into the mug and cook in the microwave for 1 minute 30 seconds at 800 watts or 1 minute 10 seconds at 1000 watts. Let it cool a little before eating.

FOR 1 MUG – 5 MINUTES (PREP + COOK)

22 *- fruit mug crumbles*

raspberry, apple & matcha tea mug crumble

FRUIT
1 apple, peeled, cored and diced
1 heaped tablespoon caster
    (superfine) sugar
a knob of butter
⅔ cup (80 g/3 oz) raspberries

CRUMBLE
1 slice of butter 5 mm
    (¼ in) thick (15 g/½ oz)
1 tablespoon soft brown sugar
2 heaped tablespoons plain
    (all-purpose) flour
1 heaped teaspoon matcha green tea
a pinch of salt

In a mug: mix the apple with the sugar and butter. Cover the mug with cling film (plastic wrap) pierced several times.

Cook in the microwave for 1 minute at 800 watts or 50 seconds at 1000 watts. Pour off any excess liquid. Add the raspberries and stir again.

In a bowl, mix the butter, soft brown sugar, flour, matcha tea and salt with your fingertips to form a dough.

Crumble it into the mug and cook in the microwave for 1 minute 30 seconds at 800 watts or 1 minute 10 seconds at 1000 watts.

Let it cool a litte before eating.

vanilla, apple & chocolate mug crumble

FRUIT
2 apples, peeled, cored and diced
1 tablespoon vanilla caster
   (superfine) sugar
a knob of butter
2 tablespoons dark chocolate chips

CRUMBLE
1 slice of butter 5 mm
   (¼ in) thick (15 g/½ oz)
1 tablespoon soft brown sugar
2 teaspoons natural vanilla extract
2 heaped tablespoons plain
   (all-purpose) flour
a pinch of salt

In a mug: mix the apple with the sugar and butter. Cover the mug with cling film (plastic wrap) pierced several times.

Cook in the microwaves for 2 minutes at 800 watts or 1 minute 30 seconds at 1000 watts. Pour off any excess liquid. Add the chocolate chips and stir again.

In a bowl, mix the butter, soft brown sugar, vanilla, flour and salt with your fingertips to form a dough.

Crumble it into the mug and cook in the microwave for 1 minute at 800 watts or 50 seconds at 1000 watts.

Let it cool a little before eating.

choc-nut & apple

mug crumble

FRUIT

1 apple, peeled,
  cored and diced
1 tablespoon caster
  (superfine) sugar
6 squares of milk chocolate,
  chopped 30 g (1 oz)
1 tablespoon single
  (light) cream

CRUMBLE

1 slice of butter 5 mm
  (¼ in) thick (15 g/½ oz)
1 tablespoon soft brown sugar
1 heaped tablespoon
  plain (all-purpose) flour
1 tablespoon chopped
  pecan nuts
1 tablespoon chopped walnuts
1 tablespoon chopped
  hazelnuts
a pinch of salt

In a mug: mix the apple with the sugar. Cover the mug with cling film (plastic wrap) pierced several times.

Cook in the microwave for 1 minute at 800 watts or 50 seconds at 1000 watts. Pour off any excess liquid. Add the chocolate and cream, stir. Cover with cling film again and cook for a further 30 seconds at 800 watts or 20 seconds at 1000 watts. Stir.

In a bowl, mix the butter, soft brown sugar, flour, the trio of nuts and salt with your fingertips to form a dough.

Crumble it into the mug and cook in the microwave for 1 minute at 800 watts or 50 seconds at 1000 watts. Let it cool a little before eating.

FOR 1 MUG – 5 MINUTES (PREP + COOK)

28 - *chocolate mug crumbles*

raspberry, apple & white chocolate mug crumble

FRUIT

1 apple, peeled, cored and diced
1 tablespoon caster (superfine) sugar
a knob of butter
generous ⅓ cup (50 g/2 oz) raspberries

CRUMBLE

1 slice of butter 5 mm
  (¼ in) thick (15 g/½ oz)
1 tablespoon soft brown sugar
2 heaped tablespoons plain
  (all-purpose) flour
1 tablespoon white chocolate chips
a pinch of salt

In a mug: mix the apple with the sugar and butter. Cover the mug with cling film (plastic wrap) pierced several times.

Cook in the microwave for 1 minute at 800 watts or 50 seconds at 1000 watts. Pour off any excess liquid. Add the raspberries and stir again.

In a bowl, mix the butter, soft brown sugar, flour, chocolate and salt with your fingertips to form a dough.

Crumble it into the mug and cook in the microwave for 1 minute at 800 watts or 50 seconds at 1000 watts.

Let it cool a little before eating.

pear & chocolate
mug crumble

FRUIT
2 pears, peeled,
  cored and diced
1 tablespoon caster
  (superfine) sugar
a knob of butter
1 tablespoon dark
  chocolate chips

CRUMBLE
1 slice of butter 5 mm
  (¼ in) thick (15 g/½ oz)
1 tablespoon soft brown sugar
3 heaped tablespoons
  plain (all-purpose) flour
1 tablespoon dark
  chocolate chips
a pinch of salt

In a mug: mix the pear with the sugar and butter.
Cover the mug with cling film (plastic wrap) pierced
several times.

Cook in the microwave for 1 minute at 800 watts or
50 seconds at 1000 watts. Pour off any excess liquid.
Add the chocolate chips and stir again.

In a bowl, mix the butter, soft brown sugar, flour, chocolate
and salt with your fingertips to form a dough.

Crumble it into the mug and cook in the microwave for
1 minute at 800 watts or 50 seconds at 1000 watts. Let it
cool a little before eating.

FOR 1 MUG – 5 MINUTES (PREP + COOK)

32 - *chocolate mug crumbles*

cherry, apple & chocolate mug crumble

FRUIT
1 apple, peeled, cored and diced
1 tablespoon caster (superfine) sugar
a knob of butter
⅓ cup (60 g/2 oz) pitted cherries

CRUMBLE
1 slice of butter 5 mm
   (¼ in) thick (15 g/½ oz)
1 tablespoon soft brown sugar
2 heaped tablespoons plain
   (all-purpose) flour
2 teaspoons unsweetened
   cocoa powder
a pinch of salt

In a mug: mix the apple with the sugar and butter. Cover the mug with cling film (plastic wrap) pierced several times.

Cook in the microwave for 1 minute at 800 watts or 50 seconds at 1000 watts. Pour off any excess liquid. Add the cherries and stir again.

In a bowl, mix the butter, soft brown sugar, flour, cocoa powder and salt with your fingertips to form a dough.

Crumble it into the mug and cook in the microwave for 1 minute at 800 watts or 50 seconds at 1000 watts.

Let it cool a little before eating.

strawberry, apple & double-choc

mug crumble

FRUIT

1 apple, peeled,
   cored and diced
1 tablespoon caster
   (superfine) sugar
a knob of butter
5 strawberries,
   rinsed and diced
1 tablespoon dark
   chocolate chips

CRUMBLE

1 slice of butter 5 mm
   (¼ in) thick (15 g/½ oz)
1 teaspoon soft brown sugar
2 tablespoons plain
   (all-purpose) flour
1 tablespoon white
   chocolate chips
a pinch of salt

In a mug: mix the apple with the sugar and butter. Cover the mug with cling film (plastic wrap) pierced several times.

Cook in the microwave for 1 minute at 800 watts or 50 seconds at 1000 watts. Pour off any excess liquid. Add the pieces of strawberry and the chocolate chips and stir.

In a bowl, mix the butter, soft brown sugar, flour, white chocolate and salt with your fingertips to form a dough.

Crumble it into the mug and cook in the microwave for 1 minute at 800 watts or 50 seconds at 1000 watts. Let it cool a little before eating.

FOR 1 MUG – 5 MINUTES (PREP + COOK)

36 - *chocolate mug crumbles*

pear with gingerbread
& white chocolate mug crumble

FRUIT

2 pears, peeled, cored and diced

1 tablespoon caster (superfine) sugar

a knob of butter

1 teaspoon gingerbread spices or
　French four-spice seasoning

1 tablespoon white chocolate chips

CRUMBLE

1 slice of butter 5 mm
　(¼ in) thick (15 g/½ oz)

1 tablespoon soft brown sugar

3 slices of gingerbread

a pinch of salt

1 tablespoon white chocolate chips

In a mug: mix the pears with the sugar and butter. Cover the mug with cling film (plastic wrap) pierced several times.

Cook in the microwave for 1 minute at 800 watts or 50 seconds at 1000 watts. Pour off any excess liquid. Add the spices, white chocolate chips and stir again.

In a bowl, mix the butter, soft brown sugar, gingerbread and salt with your fingertips to form a dough.

Crumble it into the mug and cook in the microwave for 1 minute at 800 watts or 50 seconds at 1000 watts. Sprinkle the chocolate chips over the crumble and cook for a further 30 seconds at 800 watts or 20 seconds at 1000 watts.

Let it cool a little before eating.

....

ganache mug crumble

GANACHE

6 squares of dark chocolate,
chopped (30 g/1 oz)
1 tablespoon single (light) cream

CRUMBLE

1 slice of butter 5 mm
(¼ in) thick (15 g/½ oz)
1 tablespoon soft brown sugar
2 tablespoons plain (all-purpose) flour
1 tablespoon dark chocolate chips
a pinch of salt

In a mug: mix the chocolate with the cream. Cover the mug with cling film (plastic wrap) pierced several times.

Cook in the microwave for 20 seconds at 800 watts or 10 seconds at 1000 watts. Stir and repeat the process. Stir again.

In a bowl, mix the butter, soft brown sugar, flour, chocolate chips and salt with your fingertips to form a dough.

Crumble it into the mug and cook in the microwave for 1 minute at 800 watts or 50 seconds at 1000 watts.

Let it cool a little before eating.

pear & chestnut purée

mug crumble

FRUIT

1 pear, peeled, cored and diced
2 tablespoons chestnut purée
1 tablespoon single (light) cream

CRUMBLE

1 slice of butter 5 mm (¼ in) thick (15 g/½ oz)
1 level tablespoon soft brown sugar
1 teaspoon natural vanilla extract
1 teaspoon chestnut purée
2 heaped tablespoons plain (all-purpose) flour
a pinch of salt

In a mug: cook the pear in the microwave for 1 minute 30 seconds at 800 watts or 1 minute 10 seconds at 1000 watts, covering the mug with cling film (plastic wrap) pierced several times. Pour off any excess liquid. Add the chestnut purée and the cream, then stir.

In a bowl, mix the butter, soft brown sugar, vanilla, chestnut purée, flour and salt with your fingertips to form a dough.

Crumble it into the mug and cook in the microwave for 1 minute at 800 watts or 50 seconds at 1000 watts. Let it cool a little before eating.

FOR 1 MUG – 5 MINUTES (PREP + COOK)

42 - *creamy mug crumbles*

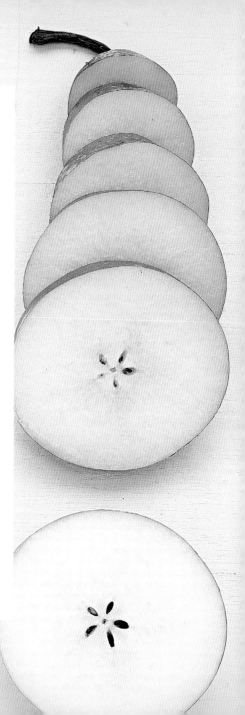

fig, apple, yoghurt & hazelnut mug crumble

FRUIT

1 apple, peeled, cored and diced

1 tablespoon caster (superfine) sugar

3 fresh figs, peeled and
cut into small pieces

1 tablespoon plain unsweetened
yoghurt

CRUMBLE

1 slice of butter 5 mm
(¼ in) thick (15 g/½ oz)

1 tablespoon soft brown sugar

1 heaped tablespoon plain
(all-purpose) flour

1 heaped tablespoon ground hazelnuts

2 tablespoons crushed hazelnuts

a pinch of salt

In a mug: cook the apple with the sugar in the microwave for 1 minute at 800 watts or 50 seconds at 1000 watts, covering the mug with cling film (plastic wrap) pierced several times. Pour off any excess liquid. Add the figs and yoghurt, then stir.

In a bowl, mix the butter, soft brown sugar, flour, hazelnuts and salt with your fingertips to form a dough.

Crumble it into the mug and cook in the microwave for 1 minute at 800 watts or 50 seconds at 1000 watts.

Let it cool a little before eating.

TIP: For an even tastier mug crumble, dry toast the hazelnuts in a frying pan for about 5 minutes.

blueberry & lemon curd

mug crumble

FRUIT
1 slice of butter 5 mm
   (¼ in) thick (15 g/½ oz)
1 small egg
juice of ½ lemon
2 tablespoons
   caster (superfine) sugar
1 teaspoon cornflour
   (cornstarch) or 50 g (2oz)
   lemon curd

1 tablespoon frozen
   blueberries

CRUMBLE
1 slice of butter 5 mm
   (¼ in) thick (15 g/½ oz)
1 heaped tablespoon
   soft brown sugar
3 tablespoons plain
   (all-purpose) flour
zest of ½ lemon

In a mug: melt the butter in the microwave. Add the egg, lemon juice, sugar and cornflour and beat. Cover the mug with cling film (plastic wrap) pierced several times.

Cook for 30 seconds at 800 watts or 20 seconds at 1000 watts (or put the lemon curd into the mug, without cooking it). Add the blueberries and stir.

Cover and cook again for 30 seconds at 800 watts or 20 seconds at 1000 watts.

In a bowl, mix the butter, soft brown sugar, flour and lemon zest with your fingertips to form a dough.

Crumble it into the mug and cook in the microwave for 1 minute at 800 watts or 50 seconds at 1000 watts.

Let it cool a little before eating.

FOR 1 MUG – 5 MINUTES (PREP + COOK)

red berries, apple, lemon & cream cheese mug crumble

FRUIT

2 tablespoons Philadelphia®
  cream cheese
juice of ½ lemon
2 teaspoons caster (superfine) sugar
1 apple, peeled, cored and diced
2 tablespoons frozen mixed red berries

CRUMBLE

1 slice of butter 5 mm
  (¼ in) thick (15 g/½ oz)
1 tablespoon soft brown sugar
3 Lotus® biscuits or other caramelised
  biscuits, crushed
1 tablespoon plain (all-purpose) flour
zest of ½ lemon

In a mug: mix the Philadelphia® cream cheese with the lemon juice and 1 teaspoon of the sugar. Add the apple, then the red berries. Sprinkle another teaspoon of sugar on top. Cover the mug with cling film (plastic wrap) pierced several times.

Cook in the microwave for 1 minute 30 seconds at 800 watts or 1 minute 10 seconds at 1000 watts. Pour off any excess liquid.

In a bowl, mix the butter, soft brown sugar, caramelised biscuits, flour and lemon zest with your fingertips to form a dough.

Crumble it into the mug and cook in the microwave for 1 minute at 800 watts or 50 seconds at 1000 watts.

Let it cool a little before eating.

banana, apple & peanut

mug crumble

FRUIT

1 apple, peeled, cored and
diced

1 tablespoon caster
(superfine) sugar

½ banana, sliced into rounds

1 heaped tablespoon
peanut butter

CRUMBLE

1 tablespoon chopped
roasted and salted peanuts

1 slice of butter 5 mm
(¼ in) thick (15 g/½ oz)

1 tablespoon soft brown sugar

2 heaped tablespoons
peanut butter

2 heaped tablespoons
plain (all-purpose) flour

In a mug: cook the apple with the sugar in the microwave
for 1 minute at 800 watts or 50 seconds at 1000 watts,
covering the mug with cling film (plastic wrap) pierced
several times. Pour off any excess liquid. Add the banana
and the peanut butter and stir.

In a bowl, mix the butter, soft brown sugar, peanut butter,
flour and peanuts with your fingertips to form a dough.

Crumble it into the mug and cook in the microwave for
1 minute at 800 watts or 50 seconds at 1000 watts. Let it
cool a little before eating.

FOR 1 MUG – 5 MINUTES (PREP + COOK)

50 - *creamy mug crumbles*

pineapple, apple & caramelised biscuit

mug crumble

FRUIT
- 1 apple, peeled, cored and diced
- 1 tablespoon vanilla sugar
- 2 slices of pineapple in syrup, cut into chunks
- 1 teaspoon ground cinnamon
- a knob of butter

CRUMBLE
- 1 slice of butter 5 mm (¼ in) thick (15 g/½ oz)
- 1 tablespoon soft brown sugar
- 2 Lotus® biscuits or other caramelised biscuits, crushed
- 1 heaped tablespoon plain (all-purpose) flour
- a pinch of salt

In a mug: mix the apple, sugar, pineapple, cinnamon and butter together. Cover the mug with cling film (plastic wrap) pierced several times.

Cook in the microwave for 1 minute at 800 watts or 50 seconds at 1000 watts. Pour off any excess liquid and stir.

In a bowl, mix the butter, soft brown sugar, caramelised biscuits, flour and salt with your fingertips to form a dough.

Crumble it into the mug and cook in the microwave for 1 minute at 800 watts or 50 seconds at 1000 watts. Let it cool a little before eating.

FOR 1 MUG – 5 MINUTES (PREP + COOK)

52 - biscuity mug crumbles

red berries, apple & shortbread

mug crumble

FRUIT
1 apple, peeled, cored and
  diced
2 tablespoons frozen
  mixed red berries
1 tablespoon caster
  (superfine) sugar
a knob of butter

CRUMBLE
1 slice of butter 5 mm
  (¼ in) thick (15 g/½ oz)
1 tablespoon soft brown sugar
2 crumbled *petits-beurre*
  or shortbread biscuits
1 heaped tablespoon
  plain (all-pupose) flour
a pinch of salt

In a mug: mix the apple with the red berries, sugar and butter. Cover the mug with cling film (plastic wrap) pierced several times.

Cook in the microwave for 1 minute at 800 watts or 50 seconds at 1000 watts. Pour off any excess liquid and stir again.

In a bowl, mix the butter, soft brown sugar, *petits-beurre* biscuits, flour and salt with your fingertips to form a dough.

Crumble it into the mug and cook in the microwave for 1 minute at 800 watts or 50 seconds at 1000 watts. Let it cool a little before eating.

FOR 1 MUG – 5 MINUTES (PREP + COOK)

54 - *biscuity mug crumbles*

damson plum & apple with Breton butter biscuits mug crumble

FRUIT
1 apple, peeled, cored and diced
3 damsons, peeled, pitted and diced
1 tablespoon caster (superfine) sugar
a knob of butter

CRUMBLE
1 slice of butter 5 mm
   (¼ in) thick (15 g/½ oz)
1 tablespoon soft brown sugar
1 heaped tablespoon plain
   (all-purpose) flour
2 Breton butter biscuits or
   galettes (cookies), crumbled
a pinch of salt
whipped cream, to serve

In a mug: mix the fruits with the sugar and butter. Cover the mug with cling film (plastic wrap) pierced several times.

Cook in the microwave for 1 minute at 800 watts or 50 seconds at 1000 watts. Pour off any excess liquid and stir again.

In a bowl, mix the butter, soft brown sugar, flour, Breton butter biscuits and salt with your fingertips to form a dough.

Crumble it into the mug and cook in the microwave for 1 minute at 800 watts or 50 seconds at 1000 watts.

Let it cool a little before eating. Serve with a spoonful of whipped cream.

mirabelle plum & shortbread

mug crumble

FRUIT
1 apple, peeled, cored and
   diced
2 mirabelle plums,
   peeled, pitted and diced
1 tablespoon caster
   (superfine) sugar
a knob of butter

CRUMBLE
1 slice of butter 5 mm
   (¼ in) thick (15 g/½ oz)
1 tablespoon soft brown sugar
2 *galettes Saint-Michel*®
   biscuits or similar thin
   butter biscuits, crumbled
1 heaped tablespoon plain
   (all-purpose) flour
a pinch of salt

In a mug: mix the apple, mirabelle plums, sugar and butter together. Cover the mug with cling film (plastic wrap) pierced several times.

Cook in the microwave for 1 minute at 800 watts or 50 seconds at 1000 watts. Pour off any excess liquid and stir again.

In a bowl, mix the butter, soft brown sugar, biscuits, flour and salt with your fingertips to form a dough.

Crumble it into the mug and cook in the microwave for 1 minute at 800 watts or 50 seconds at 1000 watts. Let it cool a little before eating.

FOR 1 MUG – 5 MINUTES (PREP + COOK)

58 - *biscuity mug crumbles*

raspberry, apple & pink-wafer biscuit

mug crumble

FRUIT
1 apple, peeled, cored and diced
1 teaspoon caster (superfine) sugar
a knob of butter
generous ⅓ cup (50 g/2 oz) raspberries

CRUMBLE
1 slice of butter 5 mm (¼ in) thick (15 g/½ oz)
1 tablespoon soft brown sugar
3 pink Reims® biscuits or similar wafer-like biscuits, crushed
1 heaped tablespoon plain (all-purpose) flour
a pinch of salt

In a mug: mix the apple with the sugar and butter. Cover the mug with cling film (plastic wrap) pierced several times.

Cook in the microwave for 1 minute at 800 watts or 50 seconds at 1000 watts. Pour off any excess liquid, add the raspberries and stir again.

In a bowl, mix the butter, soft brown sugar, biscuits, flour and salt with your fingertips to form a dough.

Crumble it into the mug and cook in the microwave for 1 minute at 800 watts or 50 seconds at 1000 watts. Let it cool a little before eating.

FOR 1 MUG – 5 MINUTES (PREP + COOK)

60 - *biscuity mug crumbles*

peach &
strawberry biscotti
mug crumble

FRUIT

1 peach, peeled, pitted and
  diced
1 tablespoon vanilla sugar
a knob of butter
5 strawberries, rinsed
  and quartered

CRUMBLE

1 slice of butter 5 mm
  (¼ in) thick (15 g/½ oz)
1 tablespoon soft brown sugar
1 tablespoon plain
  (all-purpose) flour
1 tablespoon ground almonds
2 biscotti or cake rusks,
  crumbled
a pinch of salt

In a mug: mix the peach with the sugar and butter. Cover
the mug with cling film (plastic wrap) pierced several times.

Cook in the microwave for 1 minute at 800 watts or
50 seconds at 1000 watts. Pour off any excess liquid. Add
the strawberries and stir again.

In a bowl, mix the butter, soft brown sugar, flour, ground
almonds, biscotti and salt with your fingertips to form
a dough.

Crumble it into the mug and cook in the microwave for
1 minute at 800 watts or 50 seconds at 1000 watts. Let it
cool a little before eating.

FOR 1 MUG – 5 MINUTES (PREP + COOK)

62 - biscuity mug crumbles

....

salmon with courgette & hazelnut mug crumble

SALMON & COURGETTE

150 g (5 oz) courgettes (zucchini),
   peeled and diced
100 g (3½ oz) skinless and deboned
   salmon steak, cut into chunks
a pinch of salt
1 tablespoon single (light) cream
1 teaspoon chopped dill

CRUMBLE

1 slice of butter 5 mm
   (¼ in) thick (15 g/½ oz)
10 g (½ oz) Gruyère cheese, grated
1 tablespoon ground hazelnuts
1 heaped tablespoon plain
   (all-purpose) flour
1 tablespoon chopped hazelnuts
a pinch of salt
a pinch of pepper

In a mug: cook the courgette in the microwave for 30 seconds at 800 watts or 20 seconds at 1000 watts, covering the mug with cling film (plastic wrap) pierced several times. Pour off any excess liquid.

Add the salmon, salt, cream and dill, and stir. Cover again and cook for 30 seconds at 800 watts or 20 seconds at 1000 watts. Pour off any excess liquid and stir.

In a bowl, mix the butter, Gruyère cheese, ground hazelnuts, flour, chopped hazelnuts, salt and pepper with your fingertips to form a dough.

Crumble it into the mug and cook in the microwave for 1 minute at 800 watts or 50 seconds at 1000 watts.

Let it cool a little before eating.

TIP: For an even tastier mug crumble, dry toast the hazelnuts in a frying pan for about 5 minutes.

cherry tomatoes with three cheeses mug crumble

TOMATO & CHEESE

10 cherry tomatoes, quartered
   (use only the flesh)
a pinch of salt
a pinch of pepper
1 tablespoon grated Gruyère cheese
1 slice of bleu d'Auvergne or other
   blue cheese (15 g / ½ oz)
1 tablespoon toasted pine kernels

CRUMBLE

1 slice of butter 5 mm
   (¼ in) thick (15 g / ½ oz)
1 tablespoon grated Parmesan cheese
2 heaped tablespoons wholemeal
   (whole-wheat) flour
1 teaspoon *herbes de Provence*
1 tablespoon toasted pine kernels
a pinch of salt
a pinch of pepper

In a mug: mix the tomato, salt, pepper, Gruyère, blue cheese and toasted pine kernels.

In a bowl, mix the butter, Parmesan cheese, flour, *herbes de Provence*, pine kernels, salt and pepper with your fingertips to form a dough.

Crumble it into the mug and cook in the microwave for 2 minutes at 800 watts or 1 minute 30 seconds at 1000 watts. Let it cool a little before eating.

TIP: If you can't find toasted pine kernels, dry toast some raw ones in a frying pan for 5 minutes.

courgette & feta with polenta mug crumble

COURGETTE & FETA

150 g (5 oz) courgettes (zucchini),
   peeled and diced
a pinch of salt
a pinch of pepper
1 teaspoon olive oil
2 slices of feta 1 cm (½ in) thick
   (30 g/1 oz), cut into chunks

CRUMBLE

1 slice of butter 5 mm
   (¼ in) thick (15 g/½ oz)
1 tablespoon polenta
1 heaped tablespoon plain
   (all-purpose) flour
1 teaspoon *herbes de Provence*
a pinch of salt
a pinch pepper

In a mug: cook the courgette with the salt and pepper in the microwave for 30 seconds at 800 watts or 20 seconds at 1000 watts, covering the mug with cling film (plastic wrap) pierced several times. Pour off any excess liquid. Add the olive oil and feta and stir.

In a bowl, mix the butter, polenta, flour, *herbes de Provence*, salt and pepper with your fingertips to form a dough.

Crumble it into the mug and cook in the microwave for 1 minute at 800 watts or 50 seconds at 1000 watts.

Let it cool a little before eating.

olive, tomato & Parmesan mug crumble

VEGETABLES

2 tomatoes, cut into pieces
  (use only the flesh)
6 green olives, pitted and cut in half
1 tablespoon single (light) cream
1 teaspoon chopped basil
a pinch of salt
a pinch of pepper

CRUMBLE

1 slice of butter 5 mm
  (¼ in) thick (15 g/½ oz)
1 tablespoon grated Parmesan cheese
1 tablespoon breadcrumbs
1 heaped tablespoon plain
  (all-purpose) flour
zest of ½ lemon
1 teaspoon chopped basil
a pinch of salt
a pinch of pepper

In a mug: put the tomatoes, olives, cream, basil, salt and pepper and stir.

In a bowl, mix the butter, Parmesan cheese, breadcrumbs, flour, lemon zest, basil, salt and pepper with your fingertips to form a dough.

Crumble it into the mug and cook in the microwave for 2 minutes at 800 watts or 1 minute 30 seconds at 1000 watts.

Let it cool a little before eating.

notes on the recipes

Some quantity equivalents

1 slice of butter 5 mm (¼ in) thick = 15 g (½ oz)

1 level/heaped tablespoon sugar
 = 10 g/20 g (½ oz /¾ oz)

1 level/heaped tablespoon plain (all-
 purpose) flour = 5 g/15 g (¼ oz/½ oz)

1 tablespoon chocolate chips = 10 g (½ oz)

1 teaspoon cocoa powder = 3 g (¼ oz)

1 tablespoon ground almonds = 7 g (¼ oz)

1 tablespoon chopped walnuts = 5 g (¼ oz)

1 tablespoon single (light) cream = 10 g (½ oz)

1 tablespoon honey = 10 g (½ oz)

Cooking time equivalents

1 minute at 800 watts

 = 50 seconds at 1000 watts

 = 1 minute 20 seconds at 650 watts

acknowledgements

Thanks to David and Christine for their lovely photos.
Thanks to the whole Marabout team for their trust.
Thanks to my daughters, who are great fans of *mug crumbles*
and were delighted to taste so many recipes.
And thanks to Léo for keeping me laughing!

shopping for mugs

The Conran Shop www.conranshop.co.uk

Habitat www.habitat.co.uk

Marimekko www.marimekko.com

Not On The High Street www.notonthehighstreet.com

Mug Crumbles by Christelle Huet-Gomez

© Hachette Livre (Marabout) 2015
This English language edition published in 2015 by Hardie Grant Books

Hardie Grant Books (UK)
5th & 6th Floors
52-54 Southwark Street
London SE1 1UN
www.hardiegrant.co.uk

Hardie Grant Books (Australia)
Ground Floor, Building 1
658 Church Street
Melbourne, VIC 3121
www.hardiegrant.com.au

The moral rights of Christelle Huet-Gomez to be identified as the author
of this work has been asserted by her in accordance with the
Copyright, Designs and Patents Act 1988.

Text © Christelle Huet-Gomez
Photography © David Japy

British Library Cataloguing-in-Publication Data. A catalogue record
for this book is available from the British Library.

ISBN: 978-1-78488-022-4

Publisher: Kate Pollard
Senior Editor: Kajal Mistry
Translator: Gilla Evans
Editor/Proofreader: Kay Delves
Typesetter: David Meikle
Art Direction: Christine Legeret
Photography: © David Japy

Printed and bound in China by 1010

10 9 8 7 6 5 4 3 2 1